THE MEANING OF

Wedding Anniversaries

THE MEANING OF
Wedding Anniversaries

By Gretchen Scoble and Ann Field

TEXT BY ZOË FRANCESCA

COLLAGES BY ANN FIELD

Photography by Ron Slenzak

CHRONICLE BOOKS

SAN FRANCISCO

For Matt, my true love. —GS

For Clive, my true love. —AF

Library of Congress Cataloging-in-Publication Data available.
ISBN: 0-8118-3368-2

Manufactured in China

Designed by Gretchen Scoble
Calligraphy by Elvis Swift

Distributed in Canada by Raincoast Books
9050 Shaughnessy Street
Vancouver, British Columbia V6P 6E5

10 9 8 7 6 5 4 3 2 1

Chronicle Books LLC
85 Second Street
San Francisco, California 94105

www.chroniclebooks.com

Contents

Introduction   7

The Symbols: Paper through Platinum   11

Gifts at a Glance   86

Resources   87

Acknowledgments   88

Introduction

Every anniversary celebrates a moment in the journey of marriage. The passing of another year together marks a deepening of the couple's commitment, an accumulation of time irreplaceable. To help in celebrating these occasions are special gifts, one assigned to each anniversary and each with its own material and symbolic value. In the United States, the wedding anniversary symbols begin simply, with paper and flowers, and gradually increase in substance and value. The order of gifts reflects the *investment* that the couple gives of themselves to each other. In Germany, by comparison, couples use a list of symbols that represent the progressive *strengthening* of the marriage relationship. Iron accompanies the sixty-fifth anniversary, and the venerable oak tree, the eightieth. The Victorians, so fond of cataloging and classifying, were likely the first to adapt ancient customs into a prescribed list of gifts for each wedding anniversary. It is possible that the list began as a short one, featuring only a few coveted household items, and eventually expanded to the list we know today, covering every anniversary through the seventy-fifth.

< 7 >

The anniversary couple, through a series of symbolic gifts that mark each year of their love and commitment, undertakes a journey of their own. From the first year, with its ephemeral paper gifts, to the tenth year, with its practical tins, changes occur as the partners grow to learn each other's strengths and weaknesses. The twentieth year, with its refined china, and the thirtieth year, with its glowing pearls, reflect a time of hard work and successes. In the fortieth and forty-fifth years, gemstones, with all their colorful significance, appear to guide the couple through the years of wisdom and deeper understanding. The diamond, the gift of the sixty-fifth year, colorless as glass but much more durable, is a symbol of the couple's transformation from young people with fragile dreams into mature people with a legacy of love.

For those seeking the perfect gift for their beloved or for a beloved couple, *The Meaning of Wedding Anniversaries* reveals the lore and wisdom behind the symbols and suggests ideas for gifts, both traditional and unusual. The cotton (second) anniversary, we learn, teaches a couple to stay close, and a gift of luxurious cotton sheets embodies the meaning of the symbol. Ultimately, each symbol is a gift in itself, an image from deep within our hearts that ties ancient stories to modern experiences. The meanings of wedding anniversaries are not only inspirations for gifts but a means of bringing couples closer together and helping them understand the many ways in which they can love.

< 8 >

Paper ~ 1

For the first anniversary, the fragile, transitory symbol of paper represents the delicate nature of a new relationship. The journey is just beginning. In Japan, the Shinto wedding ceremony includes sipping rice wine from a bottle decorated with paper butterflies, one male and one female. The image of the two butterflies reminds us of two lovers together in the playful honeymoon phase of their marriage. In fact, the Japanese word for paper, *kami,* also has a mystical meaning related to spirit, and folded paper streamers represent the presence of divinity.

The papyrus of ancient Egypt represented knowledge and the unfolding of life. The papyrus plant itself symbolized joy and youth, freshness and love, because it flourished as a perennial on the fertile riverbanks. Paper is also as valuable as the words written upon it; consider the *ketubah,* the Jewish marriage contract. A *ketubah* is usually handwritten by a skilled calligrapher or artist in the manner of an illuminated manuscript and is framed and hung in the couple's home.

GIFTS: *For a first anniversary, give a gift of a* ketubah, *a framed poem or love letter, or a special book. Some couples give each other tickets to a concert or show, or even a savings bond. A paper lantern symbolizes hopefulness, the light of wisdom, and the warmth of home. To emphasize the spirit of play and carefree love, offer a garland of paper flowers or an elegant package of origami papers that the couple can fold together.*

< 11 >

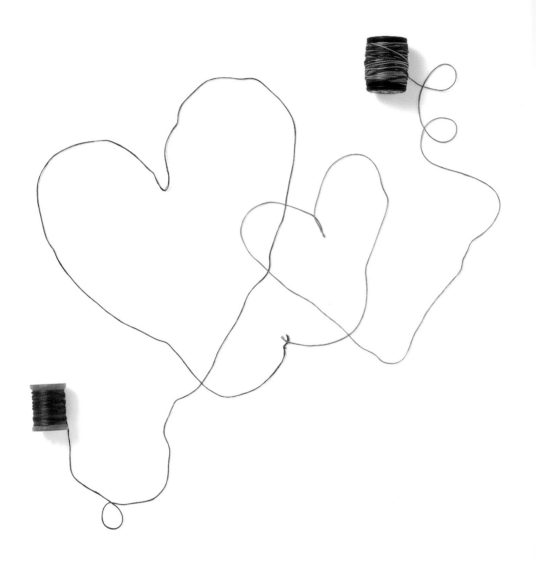

Cotton ~ 2

The delicate cotton flower needs two hundred days without frost to bloom. Nurtured by a temperate climate, the flower turns from yellow to pink to red and then falls away, allowing the fluffy pod to mature.

A couple's second anniversary, like cotton thread tied around a finger, is a reminder to recall the wedding vows and to reflect upon the maturing marriage. In Buddhist cultures, binding a string around the hands of a couple during the marriage ceremony joins them spirit to spirit and body to body. The second anniversary reminds us to reinforce the ties that bind us, and to remember those connections that first brought closeness in the relationship.

Look for patterns in your marriage, both good and bad, and think of the relationship as a fabric in which all possibilities exist. Choose wisely, and good patterns will continue to weave themselves into a strong and durable relationship.

GIFTS: *The term* thread count *refers to the number of threads in a square inch of fabric, indicating how tightly they are woven. The higher the thread count, the softer the cloth and the longer it will last. For the second anniversary, consider a gift of luxurious cotton sheets, which, like the marriage, will grow even more treasured with time.*

< 13 >

Leather ~ 3

The third wedding anniversary takes leather as its symbol. Made from the hide of animals, leather is symbolic of protection and covering. Skin is the most sensual part of our bodies and the most sensitive. Leather recalls our animal nature, the pleasures of being alive, and also our vulnerability. Our skin is what we use to experience the world, and it is the lover's familiar touch that makes marriage so comforting.

For some, leather brings up connotations of cowboys, horses, and the Wild West. For others, it conjures up biplanes and motorcycles, toughness, and freedom. And for still others, leather symbolizes all that is erotic, dangerous, and powerful. What all these images have in common is their connection to animal spirits and nature. Leather is simultaneously about safety and fantasy, and the different paths that couples may safely choose to explore their own individuality and their intimacy.

GIFTS: *For the third anniversary, give lasting leather goods such as gloves, jackets, pants, or shoes. Other options are a ranch vacation or tickets to a costume extravaganza.*

< 14 >

Fruits and *Flowers* ~ 4

From the offering of flowers on a first date to the wedding bouquet, flowers are the earth's love letters, gestures of hope and renewal. We speak of the apples and roses that bloom in each other's cheeks, and of relationships blossoming. From the Garden of Eden, where the original lovers dwelled, to the Song of Songs, which compares the beloved to roses, lilies, apples, grapes, and figs, fruits and flowers symbolize both creativity and fertility.

Flowers attract bees, butterflies, and birds with their petals and perfumes, waiting to be fertilized so fruit can grow. Flowers teach us to open ourselves to the creative process of love. Likewise, the Buddha is said to have once conducted an entire sermon by silently holding up a lotus flower to his students. With its root, stem, and blossom, the flower is complete in itself, a perfect universe and an image of the perfection to be attained.

Fruit represents immortality. The flower's seeds are hidden inside the fruit, ready to germinate and begin the cycle again. While flowers refresh our souls, fruit nourishes our bodies. Fruit offered to loved ones is a gift of health. Planting a fruit tree in your garden, especially one with beautiful or fragrant flowers, like an orange, pear, or cherry tree, is an appropriate gift for the fourth anniversary.

GIFTS: *Traditionally, the woman is represented by flowers, and the man by fruit. For the fourth anniversary, a bouquet of handpicked flowers or a basket of exotic fruits and flowers with unfamiliar scents and flavors will awaken your partner's senses. Begin a small grove of citrus or a trellis of grapes, or plant a fig tree, to symbolize fertility and health.*

< 17 >

Wood ~ 5

Forests represent a reservoir of life and mysterious knowledge, the unconscious, and wisdom. The Garden of Eden housed the tree of life, which gave immortality, and the tree of knowledge of good and evil, from which Eve plucked the fateful apple. The woods are where lovers go to be alone with each other, and where people go to meditate and worship. Legend tells us that Prince Siddhartha reached enlightenment and became the Buddha while sitting beneath the canopy of a large bo tree. In ancient times, sacred groves were dedicated to gods and goddesses, and each species of tree was known for its unique spiritual and practical gifts. There was even a form of divination known as phyllomancy—the art of telling one's fate by listening carefully to the rustle of aspen leaves.

It is said that a carpenter brings order out of chaos. The close relationship between people and trees today is evident in the frames of houses, in the frames of beds, and in the hearth. Wood symbolizes the warmth and light of sexual energy and creativity. This lively property of wood is also reflected in stories of female wood nymphs—dryads from ancient Greece and the Vrikshaka from India. In fact, the superstition of "knocking on wood" probably comes from the old tradition of invoking a tree spirit for good luck.

Wood remains one of our most precious resources. It symbolizes strength, solidity, life, and wisdom. The fifth anniversary is a milestone in a marriage. The relationship is more solid, and order is evolving out of chaos.

Gifts: *Meaningful gifts for the fifth anniversary include a carved walking stick; a piece of heirloom furniture, such as a Japanese tansu chest or a European armoire; a volunteer project at a favorite park; or a trip to a B&B with a romantic fireplace.*

< 19 >

Candy ~ 6

Candy, a symbol for all that is sweet and good in life, is the emblem of the sixth anniversary. Our love of sugar begins at the breast, mother's milk being notoriously sweet. As children, we have a voracious sweet tooth. As adults, we come to appreciate more interesting combinations, such as bitter and sweet or sweet and sour, which reflect our ability to handle life's complexities. Consider the transformation of the cocoa bean to chocolate. Naturally bitter and astringent, cocoa beans are fermented, cured, and roasted until only the kernels remain. These "nibs" are then ready to be ground, heated, and blended into chocolate. The amount of sugar and cream that is added to the nibs makes the chocolate bittersweet, semisweet, or milk.

Candy has two basic classifications: *hard* and *soft*. These terms refer to the fact that the longer sugar is boiled, the harder it gets. Between hard and soft there are at least eleven terms for the stages of boiling sugar, including *large thread, the blow, hard ball, small crack,* and *caramel*. Now translate these stages into the types of candy made from these stages: fudge, nougat, toffee, praline, peanut brittle, and butterscotch. With so many degrees of candy, how many degrees of love can a good marriage concoct?

GIFTS: *Psalm 119 says, "How sweet are your words to my taste, sweeter than honey to my mouth!" For the sixth anniversary, take your sweetie to a carnival or a country fair and indulge in caramel apples and cotton candy. Even better, go to an amusement park or circus performance in another country and see what kinds of sweets are for sale. Or stay home and sample a box of expensive chocolates flavored with spices and liqueurs.*

< 20 >

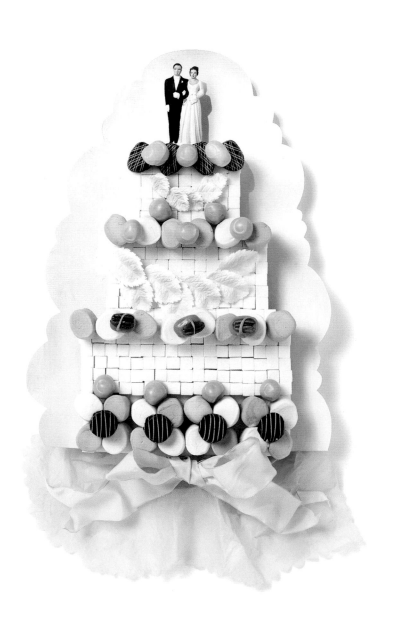

Wool ~ 7

Sheep give birth in the spring, when warmer temperatures offer lambs a greater chance of survival. The pristine lamb, with its soft, shining wool, has always symbolized hope and renewal. This, and our ancient dependence on sheep for food and clothing, connects us to the cycle of life.

In Chinese medicine, it is believed that women's bodies are governed by seven-year cycles. Thus, it is fitting that the seventh anniversary of marriage is celebrated with wool, an ancient symbol of women's work. Proverb 31 in the Old Testament says that a wife of noble character "selects wool and flax and works with eager hands . . . in her hand she holds the distaff and grasps the spindle with her fingers." Women's traditional responsibility for spinning yarn and weaving cloth for her family explains why wool was incorporated into marriage rituals, such as the custom of a Roman bride touching her new doorpost with wool.

Historically, women have used their spinning and weaving talents to make more than clothing. Mythology is filled with stories of spells and deeds being woven into tapestries, like those of the Lady of Shalott and of the Greek Fates, who spin the events of men's lives and predict the future.

GIFTS: *The Aran Islands of Ireland, known for their wool products, have a famous zigzag knit. This pattern represents the winding roads of the countryside; but it is also called the "marriage lines" because it represents the twists and turns of marriage. The gift of wool symbolizes durability, comfort, and warmth. An Aran sweater or a fine woolen blanket is the perfect gift for the seventh anniversary. A wool rug or a wool coat also makes an excellent, lasting gift.*

< 22 >

ATELIER *Pegra*

16 503

3

Bronze ~ 8

Bronze, the symbol of the eighth wedding anniversary, is partly a meditation on voice and sound. An alloy of copper and tin, bronze has been used for centuries to make gongs, bells, and cymbals. These instruments beckon people to gather, to witness, and to worship. Church bells are made of bronze, and therefore the ringing bells that announce a wedding have the distinct, sonorous voice of bronze. By the eighth anniversary, a couple will have developed the communication skills to speak clearly and honestly to each other, as well as the patience to listen and really hear.

In the Eastern Han dynasty of China, bronze was used to fashion beautifully intricate locks and keys. Locksmiths worked patterns of tigers, panthers, and butterflies into their designs. Also in that era, married women could carry keys, but unmarried women could not. Bronze is a material notorious in the making of padlocks. Ivan the Terrible, who ruled Russia in the sixteenth century, padlocked his beautiful bride in her room to protect her virtue. Perhaps it is this story that made the padlock a popular symbol for a "prisoner of love."

The Bronze Age started sometime around 1,000 B.C. when people first learned to blend metals. Even today, sculptors prefer bronze for casting because it flows evenly into nooks and crannies. A couple's love for each other must flow into every aspect of the relationship, not just the places where it's easiest to love.

GIFTS: *Gifts appropriate for the eighth anniversary include bronze jewelry, chimes or bells made with bronze, a guided tour of a Bronze Age art collection, or enrollment in a metalworking or sculpture class.*

< 24 >

Pottery ~ 9

In the Bible and the Koran, as in other stories of creation, much is said about humans being created from clay. Shapeless and hard at first, once clay is moistened with water, it can be molded into any form. The clay represents the flesh, while the water represents the soul.

Gathered and shaped by hand, clay produced the first vessels used to carry water and store food. Clay pots were once an integral part of domestic and married life, and distinctive markings on ancient pottery bespeak the civilizations from whence they came. In the American Southwest, Native Americans uphold the tradition of the "wedding vase." This ornamental ceramic jug has a loop handle and two spouts. During the marriage ceremony, the bride and groom drink water (or, symbolically, nectar) from the spouts, sometimes passing the jug to other members of the wedding party. After the wedding, the vase is kept in the home as both a reminder of the ceremony and an object of art.

GIFTS: *For the ninth anniversary, a gift of an artisan ceramic vase, bowl, or set of mugs is appropriate. A bowl will symbolize fertility, while other shapes will simply betoken the home of the couple as a warm and nurturing place.*

< 27 >

Tin ~ 10

The milestone of the tenth wedding anniversary is represented by tin, a gleaming and malleable metal. Once precious to alchemists and astrologers, tin was known by the code name of Jupiter and was an important component in the search for gold and immortality.

Tin did achieve an immortality of sorts in 1810, when Peter Durand patented the tin-plated iron can for preserving food. Tin protected the iron from corrosion, enabling the food or liquid within the can to last indefinitely. In 1974, American chemists analyzed canned foods from the *Bertrand,* a steamboat that sunk in the Missouri River in 1865 on its way to provision Montana gold miners. The brandied peaches, oysters, plum tomatoes, and honey were still perfectly preserved, 109 years later.

Toys made of tin had their heyday from the mid-nineteenth through the mid-twentieth centuries. Miniature automobiles and trains; carousels and Ferris wheels; robots and rockets mimicked the industrial and scientific revolutions taking place around them. Today, tinplate toys from Germany, France, England, and Japan are considered highly collectible items.

GIFTS: *The tin anniversary has a theme of preservation and longevity. Although tin itself is a soft metal (only lead is softer), it forms alloys with other metals like silver, iron, and copper, creating durable goods of pewter or bronze. For the tenth anniversary, gifts of pewter tableware or collectible tin windup toys are perfect. So is sheet music from Tin Pan Alley greats like Irving Berlin, Cole Porter, George Gershwin, Jerome Kern, Lerner and Loewe, or Richard Rodgers.*

< 28 >

Steel ~ 11

On the surface, the symbol of the eleventh anniversary stands for our domestic prowess. After all, steel is found throughout the home, in kitchen sinks and appliances, bathroom faucets, window frames, and even roofs. Steel, an alloy of iron and carbon, speaks to the strength of a good partnership. Stainless steel, rustproof and resistant to corrosion, exemplifies notions of permanency and durability. "To steel oneself" is to prepare, fortify, and get ready.

On a deeper level, grace, as strength, derives from steel: the union of iron and carbon gives steel unique musical qualities. Steel instruments are popular in the Western Hemisphere, from Trinidad, in the Caribbean, where steel drums originated, to Hawaii, where steel guitars were invented. In the "sacred steel" tradition in the United States, steel guitars are coaxed into sounding like human voices in prayerful song.

GIFTS: *For the eleventh anniversary, gifts might include a new set of cooking knives for the household chef, tickets to a concert, a trip to Hawaii or Trinidad, or a tour of an old steel mill that has been converted into a museum of American history.*

< 30 >

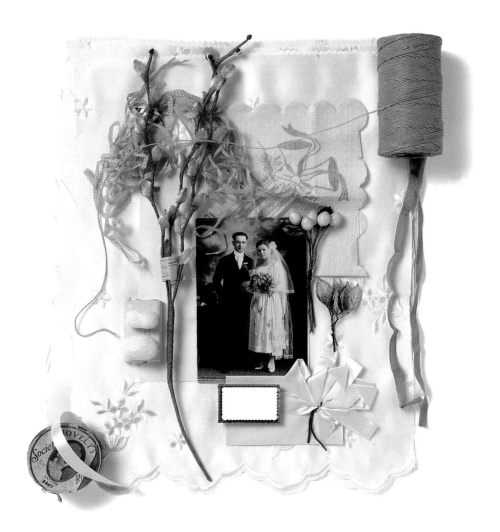

Silk ~ 12

In 1946, Betty Green was married in a dress made from a silk parachute. Her fiancé, Edwin Morgan Jr., had brought the parachute back from Germany, where he'd fought in World War II. The image of the parachute wedding gown embodies the complexity of silk: it is at once fiercely strong and incredibly soft.

Although many insects spin silk, the silk we wear comes from the Chinese *Bombyx mori* silkworm, which feeds exclusively on mulberry leaves. To build its cocoon, the silkworm spins silk from glands near its head. Workers carefully unwrap these cocoons—up to three thousand feet of silk filament can be obtained from each one. The most romantic form of silk is dupioni, produced when two silkworms spin a double cocoon together, from which they will both emerge as moths.

GIFTS: *For the twelfth anniversary, give silk pajamas, an exquisite pillow made from kimono silk, an inscribed copy of Alessandro Baricco's novel* Silk, *a musical offering from the Silk Road Project, or a trip to China or India.*

< 33 >

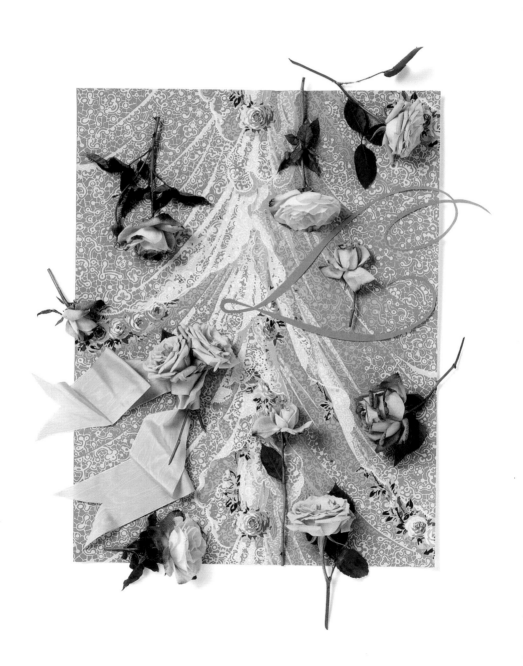

Lace ~ 13

Lace is admired as much for what it isn't as for what it is. The beauty of lace lies in the empty spaces between the knots, called "openwork." For the thirteenth anniversary, lace evokes painstaking attention to detail—but also the breathing spaces and open moments that make a work of beauty. In *The Delicacy and Strength of Lace,* a book of letters between the poets Leslie Marmon Silko and James Wright, Wright wrote, "Sometimes I wonder about things like lace, things that human beings make with their own hands, things that aren't much help as shelter from the elements or against war or other kinds of brutality. . . . Nevertheless, the art continues to survive." Silko replied, "Your letter with the lace . . . brought me somehow to blossoming trees, so white I can think only of a snowstorm, and how vulnerable . . . the budded trees are in late winter storms." Silko was right. The inspiration for lace patterns is taken from flowers, plants, snowflakes, and other natural forms. Different types of lace are named for the regions they originated in, such as Chantilly, Alençon, Venetian, Duchesse, and Maltese.

GIFTS: *Thirteenth-anniversary gifts include table linens, a framed piece of antique lace, a trip to a famous lace-making region in Europe, or a microscope for viewing snowflakes and other hidden secrets of nature.*

< 35 >

Agate ~ 14

Agates were once used as talismans to bring good luck and ward off the evil eye. The Book of Exodus describes a sacred breastplate mounted with twelve gems that gives its wearer decision-making powers. Of the twelve gems—which represent the twelve tribes of Israel—at least half are agates or closely related stones (jasper, onyx, chrysolite, jacinth, turquoise, and beryl). Moss agate features fernlike patterns, while other agates have fossils embedded in them. Ranging in color from chocolate brown to red to gray, agates often feature bands similar to tree rings, with an "eye" in the middle.

Presenting someone with an agate acknowledges the preciousness of differing opinions and perspectives, and an agate also serves as a symbolic talisman of watchfulness, luck, and protection.

GIFTS: *For the fourteenth anniversary, give a carved agate bowl or other object made from agate. Some collectors prefer simple, polished agates. The most famous region in the world for agate crafting is Idar-Oberstein in Germany. In the United States, Oregon, Washington, Idaho, Montana, and Nebraska are noted for their agate deposits. A journey to an agate region makes for an adventure in geology and a grand introduction to gemstones.*

< 37 >

Crystal ~ 15

Both naturally occurring quartz crystal and glass transformed by the addition of lead oxide are known to us as crystal. The crystal used for authentic crystal balls, alternative healing, and electronics is quartz crystal. The crystal used for stemware and chandeliers is glass mixed with lead oxide. Whether quartz or glass, what makes crystal special is its qualities of clarity and transparency, the symbols of the fifteenth wedding anniversary.

When tapped or gently rubbed, crystal glasses make such beautiful sounds that Benjamin Franklin was inspired to invent an instrument called the glass armonica out of his own wine goblets. The musical property of crystal is also found in the singing sands of beaches and deserts in places such as Hawaii, Japan, and Saudi Arabia. Every material has a natural frequency at which it vibrates, called a resonant frequency. When two people are in tune with each other, they create a natural harmony.

GIFTS: *The crystal anniversary is also special from a material standpoint because it marks the first anniversary when expensive items are introduced as gifts. However, the qualities of crystal can be expressed and celebrated in many ways. A journey to hear singing sands at a remote beach, a look into a real crystal ball, or a more traditional gift of wine glasses or a crystal clock are all good possibilities.*

< 39 >

Peridot ~ 16

Bright olive green in color, peridot forms under the intense heat and pressure of volcanic activity. Peridot is found wherever there are volcanoes—places like Vesuvius, Myanmar, Hawaii, Arizona, Egypt, and Pakistan. Often mistaken for emeralds, peridots are only semiprecious gems. Peridot's lesson, however, is very valuable. Out of conflict, fire, and explosive conditions can emerge a beautiful and vivid reminder of the strength of love.

Peridot can withstand high heat because it has already survived a trial by fire. In addition to its value for jewelry, peridot is used in the manufacture of firebricks. Sometimes called an "extraterrestrial" gem, peridot is also found in meteors that fall to earth from outer space—a reminder that we are not isolated beings but are connected to the stars and the universe as much as we are connected to each other through fate and through love.

GIFTS: *A traditional sixteenth-anniversary gift is an earthly or extraterrestrial peridot gemstone set in gold for a ring, earrings, or other adornment. (Gold settings are historically appropriate for peridot, which is associated with the sun and fire.) A trip to a volcanic region like Oahu, Arizona, or Egypt would work, too. The island of Zabargad in the Red Sea is the most famous historical location for peridot. Another good destination would be the Cologne Cathedral in Germany. In 1163, Christian crusaders brought back large peridot stones that later became glorious decorations for the cathedral's focal Shrine of the Three Holy Magi.*

< 40 >

Watches ~ 17

Small enough to carry in the pocket or on the wrist, watches allow each person to keep his or her own personal time. Watches first came into use in the form of pocket-sized sundials in the tenth century A.D. In the sixteenth century, watches with a spring mechanism were worn as pendants (for women) or in pockets (for men). Wristwatches for women came into use in the nineteenth century, but it wasn't until World War I that wristwatches for men grew popular.

As personal timekeepers, watches help us with more than being prompt. Most clocks and watches are round in shape, symbolizing time's cyclical nature. The concept of time as a wheel reflects early human attempts to gauge time by the movement of the stars, moon, and planets. The zodiac, originally created to mirror the constellations, has twelve signs, and our clocks have twelve hours. A watch reminds us that in the circle of the days of the week and the cycle of the seasons, we always have new chances to begin again, to do or say the thing we didn't do or say before.

GIFTS: *When quartz crystals were adapted for watches in 1970, battery-driven watches replaced the old mechanical watches. Still, operational antique watches are easy to find. Give a watch that fits the recipient's personality: a pocket watch for someone who adores history, a jeweled watch for someone who enjoys elegant occasions, a sports watch for an adventurer. Astrological charts, astronomical devices such as telescopes, and electronic calendars are also appropriate.*

< 43 >

Cat's-Eye ~ 18

A true cat's-eye is made of the mineral chrysoberyl. Cat's-eyes are yellow, green, or brown. When held at an angle, they reveal a narrow band of light similar to a feline pupil contracting in the sun, a quality called chatoyancy. Dear to cat lovers, the cat's-eye represents vision and insight, qualities vital to an experienced couple. A cat's pupils expand much farther than do those of human eyes, allowing them to see even by starlight. The tapetum lucidum, a membrane lining the back of a cat's retina, makes its eyes seem to glow in the dark.

Ancient Egyptians equated cats with fertility, the home, dancing, music, and joy. The cat goddess Bast kept the darkness, in the form of a serpent, under her paw during the daytime. For their eighteenth anniversary, a couple celebrates their deepening insight—into each other, and the world around them.

GIFTS: *Offer a pendant or ring featuring a cat's-eye gemstone, or a statuette of the cat goddess Bast. A kitten will literally bring cat's-eyes into your home, as well as a source of amusement.*

< 45 >

Aquamarine ~ 19

Aquamarine, the blue variety of the mineral beryl, is named for the sea. Literally, the word *aquamarine* means "sea water." Mined in Madagascar and Myanmar, the stones are in fact as blue as the sea, and many have a faint green light reminiscent of sparkling waves. The poet Yeats compared aquamarines to the color of unicorns' eyes. Dreamy, spiritual, and flowing, the aquamarine anniversary is an occasion to fall deeper in love.

Aquamarines are said to be the treasured gems of mermaids. These sirens with flowing hair and shimmering fishtails are descended from Aphrodite and from even more ancient goddesses of the sea and moon. In symbolic terms, the ocean is associated with the unconscious, intuition, and procreation. The woman in the marriage is like the mermaid, a lover calling to the sailor to abandon his ship—that is, his intellect—and join her in the sea, the place of emotion.

GIFTS: *Aquamarine lore refers specifically to married couples. It's said that the gem helps couples settle their differences and come closer together. For the nineteenth anniversary, indulge in a fantasy world where unicorns and mermaids are real. While presenting a gift of an aquamarine ring, earrings, or pendant, read aloud from Edmund Spenser or William Butler Yeats.*

< 46 >

China ~ 20

China is another name for porcelain, a ceramic that, at its finest, is a marriage of kaolin clay and the mineral feldspar. Like yin and yang, kaolin and feldspar go hand in hand. Mixed together at high temperatures, the two produce beautiful and durable ceramics. It is said that when fine porcelain breaks, the glaze is indistinguishable from the body.

In China, the country where porcelain was first manufactured, the image of two mandarin ducks, one male and one female, grace porcelain ware for newlyweds and married couples. Mandarin duck pairs are known for their fidelity to each other. Kaolin and feldspar, drake and duck: the twentieth anniversary is about lasting pairs.

GIFTS: *One might give a table setting made of porcelain, a porcelain tea set, or a porcelain vase or keepsake box (such as an antique snuffbox). Or take a trip to an Asian garden, museum, or tea ceremony.*

< 48 >

Brass ~ 21

Anything but shy, the brass anniversary announces itself with a fanfare of trumpets. The couple, having made it through twenty-one years together, has caught the brass ring of happiness. The lucky brass ring on the carousel is actually a symbol that dates back to fifteenth-century France. Testing his skill and horsemanship, an experienced knight would attempt to catch a small, dangling ring on his lance while his horse ran at a full gallop.

The word *carousel,* meaning "little war," originated in a war game of the twelfth century. Soldiers in training tossed hollow balls filled with perfume back and forth to one another while on horseback. He who missed and dropped the ball would reek of perfume afterward. The spirit of these games is reflected in *brass* used as a noun: "a person or thing worth catching"; *brassy* describes a personality trait: audacious, bold, brazen.

GIFTS: *Give the gift of a miniature or life-sized carousel horse, a music box, brass candlesticks, or a brass chandelier. For ninety cents plus the cost of airfare and hotel, offer a ride on the beautiful 1908 carousel in New York City's Central Park.*

< 50 >

Copper ~ 22

Copper is closely linked to Venus, the goddess of love. The pictorial symbol for copper and the symbol for the planet Venus are the same. The people of Cyprus, where copper mining flourished in classical, Hellenistic, and Roman times, worshiped Venus. The word *copper* comes from the name Cyprus, and even today, the symbol of Venus is used on maps to indicate copper mines.

As anyone with copper cookware knows, polished copper has a special glow that reflects a warm light into the home. Copper conducts heat and electricity, and its malleability allows it to be shaped into even the thinnest of wires without breaking.

When exposed to moist air, copper naturally develops a green coating, or patina. The greenish-blue color of this patina, called verdigris, is highly prized by artists and sculptors. A true patina comes only with time and exposure to the elements. Although it's popular nowadays to create an artificial patina, the couple celebrating twenty-two years together has, over the decades, achieved the real thing.

GIFTS: *For the twenty-second anniversary, a trip to Cyprus—specifically Paphos, the birthplace of Venus—is in order. For the homebody, give a copper kettle. A sensual meal will surely spark the fires of love and affection. A fire in the hearth or a bonfire on the beach can also be an expression of warmth.*

< 53 >

Silver Plate ~ 23

The twenty-third anniversary is marked by the reflective qualities of silver light, the same qualities that once made silver popular for mirrors and early photography. These impressions, captured in space and time, give the twenty-third anniversary its contemplative mood. Mirrors are how we see ourselves; photographs are how another eye sees us. For a couple married for twenty-three years, each partner serves as both the other's mirror and their camera. They see each other in a "silver" light, each recording years of memories and impressions layered beneath current images.

In eighteenth-century England, a craftsman named Thomas Boulsover found a way to imitate silver tableware by fusing silver to copper. Two thin sheets of silver fused onto either side of a sheet of copper could be rolled and formed into hollowware, in which the copper showed only at the seams. This was the beginning of silver plating, an art that brought a taste of luxury to ordinary people. A hundred years later, Henry and George Elkington patented a method for electroplating, and in 1868, Queen Victoria started a trend whereby members of European royalty allowed their silver objects to be copied in silver plate for wider distribution. In joining the repertoire of domestic objects, silver plate elevated family life to a grander scale, making precious heirlooms available to even the common man.

GIFTS: *Research the family silver pattern and replace missing pieces. Find an antique silver-backed mirror. Create or pose for a modern-day daguerreotype, or purchase a collectible antique daguerreotype. For those with a sense of humor, give replicas of William Hogarth's 1745* Marriage à la Mode *prints, originally engraved on silver plates.*

< 54 >

Musical Instruments ~ 24

Sometimes words don't come easily; that's when music comes into play. Instruments are a medium through which deeply felt emotions can be expressed on a nonverbal level. The twenty-fourth anniversary is a good time to take up an instrument, share dance lessons, play or listen to duets, or add to a collection of music.

In 1914, Curt Sachs and E. M. von Hornbostel devised a classification system for all musical instruments. The five main classes of instruments they identified are idiophones (instruments that have their own sonorous qualities, such as rattles, gongs, and bells); membranophones (percussion instruments, such as drums); aerophones (reed and wind instruments); chordophones (stringed instruments); and electrophones (instruments that depend on electrical vibrations or amplifiers). Musicians know that each instrument, like each person, has its own characteristic voice and expressions. This year, celebrate what Walt Whitman called the "Proud Music of the Storm" in his classic volume *Leaves of Grass*:

> *A festival song!*
> *The duet of the bridegroom and the bride—a marriage-march,*
> *With lips of love, and hearts of lovers, fill'd to the brim with love;*
> *The red-flush'd cheeks, and perfumes—the cortege swarming,*
> *   full of friendly faces, young and old,*
> *To flutes' clear notes, and sounding harps' cantabile.*

GIFTS: *Give tickets to a concert of favorite music or by a favorite musician. Compose a song. For musicians, this is the perfect year for the gift of a superior instrument.*

< 56 >

Silver ~ 25

Like Beethoven's famous Moonlight Sonata, the twenty-fifth anniversary is an understated triumph of romantic passion. Silver is used as shorthand for all things precious yet now within reach: silver dollars, silver chains, silver spoons. For the anniversary couple, silver is about the mastery of one's craft and attainment of material wealth.

Silver is one of the oldest metals used for ornamentation. The ancient Egyptians, Phoenicians, Minoans, Byzantines, Persians, Indians, and Tibetans all had their prized silversmiths. The silver-anniversary husband and wife are like two artisans of the craft and technique of love. For them, the technique of filigree refers to the myriad important details they know about each other. Repoussé is the way they leave their mark on each other. Chasing is the art of creating an impression on the world around them.

GIFTS: *Sterling-silver objects make excellent gifts for the twenty-fifth anniversary. An original work by a silversmith is perfect for the occasion. Silver bracelets with fine workmanship, or a silver teapot, serving plate, or candelabra, are other possibilities. Travelers might also appreciate a trip to Mexico, where silver has a long history, or a journey to London to view silver museum pieces.*

< 59 >

Original Art ~ 26

The twenty-sixth anniversary is focused on perception. When artists set out to portray a scene, a person, or an emotion, their heart, mind, and eye work in concert to record what they perceive. For the twenty-sixth-anniversary couple, original art represents that complete act of perception—not only of the world around them but of the truth in each other.

The same way that a live concert touches us differently from recorded music, an original painting, drawing, or photograph on the wall holds more significance than a reproduction. The mark of the artist's hand is there, bringing us that much closer to the piece and to the awareness of one's own power to influence perception and reality. For the anniversary couple, original art is a reminder that perception and authenticity are the qualities that make a marriage great rather than just good.

GIFTS: *Throughout time, many famous couples have collected art with united focus and passion. Henry "Hunk" and Mary Margaret "Moo" Anderson began collecting in the 1960s, and in 2000 their collection was billed as the highlight of the San Francisco Museum of Modern Art's exhibition schedule. Herbert and Dorothy Vogel, a New York postal worker and a librarian, collect cutting-edge modern art; their collection has been exhibited at the National Gallery and at museums around the United States. A testimony to the uniqueness of the relationship, original art is a perfect gift for a couple to exchange on their twenty-sixth anniversary.*

< 61 >

ROMA – A. CANOVA – PAOLINA BORGHESE
DETTAGLIO (MUSEO BORGHESE)

Sculpture ~ 27

I sometimes wonder if the hand is not more sensitive to the beauties of sculpture than the eye. I should think the wonderful rhythmical flow of lines and curves could be more subtly felt than seen. Be that as it may, I know that I can feel the heartthrobs of the ancient Greeks in their marble gods and goddesses. —Helen Keller

Classical sculptures stand as monuments to human ideals.

Among the Seven Wonders of the World are the statues of the Olympian Zeus and the Colossus of Rhodes. Ralph Waldo Emerson said, "I look on Sculpture as history. I do not think the Apollo and the Jove impossible in flesh and blood. Every trait the artist recorded in stone, he had seen in life, and better than his copy." Whether a sculpture is representational, like Rodin's *Orpheus and Eurydice,* or abstract, like Henry Moore's *Reclining Figure,* the beholder longs to experience the work of art through touch.

A sculptor confronts the raw material of wood, stone, clay, or metal and forms a relationship with it, pondering, and eventually pulling shape from the shapeless, extracting meaning and beauty in the most personal way.

For the married couple, sculpture can symbolize tangible form, attention to the body, and the lover's physical presence. A gift of sculpture can remind us that no matter how temporary the flesh, permanence lies in the universal fact that through the body we all experience life and each other.

GIFTS: *The anniversary couple might make a visit to a famous sculpture garden, like the Isamu Noguchi Garden Museum on the island of Shikoku, Japan; Sculpture by the Sea in Sydney, Australia; Sculpture at Goodwood in West Sussex, England; or one of many other sculpture parks and gardens worldwide. The gift of an original sculpture is a beautiful gesture.*

< 63 >

Orchids ~ 28

As the first living, breathing anniversary gift since the fruits and flowers of the fourth anniversary, orchids hint at a second honeymoon. To many minds, orchids are the supreme flowers of sensuality and beauty. Some thirty thousand species of orchids grow in both of the world's hemispheres. Charles Darwin was fascinated by the infinite ways in which orchids deploy form and color to ensure pollination. Orchids symbolize variety, inventiveness, adaptation, and regeneration—all in the name of love.

In nature, orchids grow almost anywhere, even on air. Pure vanilla, one of the most sensual and welcoming smells we have, comes from the seedpods of a certain type of orchid. The Aztecs discovered the magical combination of vanilla and cocoa to form a precious substance: chocolate. They incorporated orchids into religious rituals and gave symbolic meanings to various orchids that grew in the wild. In Hawaii, brides wear crowns of orchids. In China, orchids are one of the Four Noble Flowers.

GIFTS: *A second honeymoon to Mexico, Hawaii, China, or another location famous for its native orchids is perfect. A renewal of wedding vows would also be in order this year, with fragrant orchids as a backdrop. Give potted orchids or high-quality chocolate made with pure vanilla.*

< 65 >

Furniture ~ 29

Interior designers use the words *harmony, balance, symmetry, dialogue,* and *unity* to describe the ways in which a beautiful room combines form and function. It's no coincidence that the same words describe good marriages. In design terms, colors, textures, shapes, and patterns are all taken into consideration when making a home feel truly pleasant and comfortable. Enjoyable routines, shared tasks, and unexpected kindnesses are some of the equivalent details of a marriage that help form a good living space. The twenty-ninth anniversary, traditionally celebrated with new furniture, marks an opportunity for the married couple to take a fresh look at their nest.

The earliest furniture in history consisted of beds, stools, tables, and storage chests. Today, we use furniture for the same reasons: a cozy spot for resting or eating, and a safe place to store our belongings. Despite these mundane functions, every piece of furniture takes on a mysterious significance once it enters our home and becomes ours. The bed represents intimacy; the table represents nourishment and fulfillment. The styles we choose reflect more than our economic status; they reflect our image of sanctuary.

It is only one's thoughts that fill a room with something more than furniture.
—Wallace Stevens

GIFTS: *Together or individually, a couple might purchase a new piece of furniture or an antique. Or they could arrange for a meeting with a decorator, a feng shui consultation, a visit to a furniture studio or museum, or a paid appraisal of the contents of their home.*

< 66 >

Pearl ~ 30

The thirtieth anniversary is like a full moon on a hot summer night: radiant, soft, and iridescent. The moon, reflected on the water's surface, is enclosed again, deep beneath the surface, in pearls. Pearls represent hidden beauty, purity, and depths of emotion and understanding. In the parlance of literature, the pearl signifies precious innocence. The pearl has no guile; it simply exists, hidden within its shell, until discovered.

Pearls are the only gems that aren't stones. Made of crystalline forms of calcium carbonate with conchiolin, they grow inside bivalve mollusks like oysters and mussels. They can grow in salt water or fresh water, rivers as well as oceans. Maybe because of pearls' unusual stature, somewhere between animal and mineral, people have sometimes spoken of them as "alive," capable of changing color, temperature, and mood.

Pearls are associated with women not only because of famous pearl fanciers like Cleopatra, Queen Elizabeth I, and Elizabeth Taylor, but also because of the *ama* pearl divers in Japan—generations of women who have dived for pearls, dressed all in white. Pearls have also made traditional wedding gifts for young brides. Pearls are not, however, restricted to women. Native American Powhatan men were seen wearing pearl earrings and necklaces by early European visitors, as were men of Indian nobility.

GIFTS: *A woman might appreciate a present of a pearl necklace or pearl earrings. For a more lavish gift, book a trip to a pearl-producing country, such as Japan or Bahrain. You can also find rare editions of books on pearls from China, ancient Greece, or Elizabethan England. Or you can go beyond the pearl to its source: oysters are famous for their aphrodisiac qualities. Choose the freshest, smallest oysters possible.*

< 69 >

Jade ~ 35

Confucian and Taoist scholars of China's Chou dynasty credited jade with qualities ranging from wisdom to moral superiority, and with powers including self-protection and immortality. In an even more distant past, carved jade amulets accompanied people of the Shang dynasty to the afterlife. A practice begun in those times, and continued to this day, is that of carving jade into the symbols for the spirits of heaven *(pi)* and earth *(ts'ung)*. *Pi* is depicted as a round, flat disk with a circle or a square carved out in the center; *ts'ung* is a cylinder revealing a square cross-section. Similarly, the thirty-fifth anniversary is about carving out a place of protection, virtue, and immortality for the couple.

Nephrite and jadeite are the two accepted forms of jade. Nephrite (called *yu* in Chinese) is the gem revered in China since ancient times. Jade pendants, earrings, and bracelets are typical wedding gifts in China. Jadeite *(fei-tsui* in Chinese, after the kingfisher bird's plumage) was carved and treasured in the ancient Americas by the Olmec and Mayan peoples, and is the more rare and valuable form of jade. Connoisseurs compare the feel of polished jade to the texture of a beautiful woman's skin. Although jade comes in many colors, the clearer and brighter green a piece of jade is, the greater its value.

GIFTS: *A jade pendant or freestanding jade carving makes a simple gift. Or arrange for a trip to the Liangzhu Culture Museum in Yuhang City, China, to see Neolithic nephrite carvings, or to Guatemala, where vast, ancient jadeite quarries have been discovered. A gift of green tea ("liquid jade") is symbolic; the bibliophile might enjoy a copy of the* Shi jing *(Book of odes), a collection of songs from the Chou dynasty.*

< 70 >

Ruby ~ 40

Celestial ruby is another name for the alchemists' philosophers' stone, or "elixir of life." Red is the color of valor and the color of blood; it is blood that tints the cheeks and lips of the beloved. In ancient Rome, as in traditional China, red was the chosen color for brides. The fortieth anniversary takes pride and courage from love.

Rubies are a form of the mineral corundum, the second-hardest mineral after the diamond. Corundum is found in South Asia, where, in Thailand and in Myanmar, the word for *ruby* is also the word for *pomegranate*. Those who believe that rubies, like fruit, ripen until their red color is at its deepest mark this kinship of rubies and fruit. Seemingly alive, rubies glow with warmth, fire, and life. On the fortieth anniversary, love is celebrated in boldest display, as in E. H. Whinfield's translation of Omar Khayyám's Rubáiyát poems:

> *Wine is a melting ruby, cup its mine;*
> *Cup is the body, and the soul is wine;*
> *These crystal goblets smile with ruddy wine. . . .*
> *Drink wine! 'tis life etern, and travail's meed,*
> *Fruitage of youth, and balm of age's need:*
> *'Tis the glad time of roses, wine, and friends;*
> *Rejoice thy spirit—that is life indeed.*

GIFTS: *Traditionally, gifts of ruby gemstones are set in gold. Wine-loving couples will enjoy a rare red wine or port, and ruby-red goblets to drink it from. A trip to Myanmar, Thailand, or Sri Lanka would be appropriate—especially to the Valley of Rubies, in Myanmar. More simply, one might present his or her beloved with an illustrated edition of Omar Khayyám's Rubáiyát poems.*

< 72 >

Sapphire ~ 45

From yon blue heaven above us bent,
The gardener Adam and his wife
Smile at the claims of long descent.
—Lord Alfred Tennyson

The sapphire is as serenely blue as the sky, indicating a cool contrast to the heat of the ruby. Oddly, both are forms of corundum, and rubies and sapphires are distinguishable by color alone. Sapphires come in all shades of blue, just as the sky changes from hour to hour as it refracts light. Blue is associated with loyalty, faithfulness, and meditation. For the forty-fifth-anniversary couple, sapphires communicate honor, inspiration, and serendipity.

The word *sapphire* comes from the Hebrew for "precious stone." Sapphires are found in Kashmir, Sri Lanka, Myanmar, India, and Thailand. Many of the most beautiful and famous sapphires found in Kashmir between 1882 and 1887 came into the hands of royalty in India and in faraway Europe. One example, the St. Edward's Sapphire, now adorns the imperial state crown of Britain.

GIFTS: *Sapphire jewelry, or the gift of an open, clear-blue sky followed by a night sky sparkling with stars, is something that can be truly appreciated only from a prairie, an open desert, or a boat.*

< 74 >

Gold ~ 50

Gold is the color of dawn and the color of sunset, the closest thing on earth to the sun's brilliance, shine, and color. The ancient civilizations of the Sumerians, Mayans, Aztecs, Etruscans, Nubians, Egyptians, Minoans, and Celts were famed for their beautiful gold objects. Used for ceremonial rituals and protective amulets, gold was the physical representation of the power of the sun. During the centuries of transition when gold was transformed from a religious symbol into a monetary one, vast quantities of gold were stolen, melted down, shipwrecked, hidden, or lost.

The fiftieth anniversary is the pot of gold at the end of the rainbow: the reward for a happy life together. The golden anniversary is truly a golden year, representing the mystery and adventure of marriage, and offering a call to a more refined, more perfect understanding of love.

GIFTS: *The value of gold is the stuff of legend. Civilizations rise and fall, but the value of gold shines through. A couple at their fiftieth anniversary has truly earned the gift of gold. A tray of Indian desserts decorated with gold leaf, a trip to sun temples in Central America or India, or a lavishly illustrated book on alchemy will acknowledge this. For the ultimate tribute, plan a reaffirmation of wedding vows, with gold rings and large bouquets of golden flowers.*

< 76 >

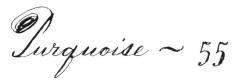

Turquoise ~ 55

The fifty-fifth anniversary speaks to the concept of oasis and sanctuary. The message for the couple who has reached this milepost is this: be each other's oasis in the desert; be the patch of blue sky and the spring of clear water for each other to cherish. The poet Scott Momaday, of Kiowa Native American descent, wrote these lines:

> *Earth and I gave you turquoise*
> *when you walked singing*
> *We lived laughing in my house*
> *and told old stories.*

Turquoise exists in the desert—but only where there is water. Because of its unique and startling color, turquoise was prized by many ancient civilizations for use in sculpture, mosaic works, jewelry, and architecture. In contemplating the smooth, earthy feel of turquoise, visualize the Bibi Khan Mosque, with its turquoise cupola, built by Timur for his wife in fourteenth-century Samarkand. Picture the four turquoise bracelets found on the arm of Queen Zer, or the carved serpent with its turquoise mosaic that belonged to Montezuma II. Imagine the native people of Chaco Canyon, who exchanged pieces of turquoise for the feathers of tropical birds.

GIFTS: *Give keepsake rings of turquoise; after all, turquoise is still popular for wedding rings in Russia, and in Europe it means "forget me not." An item of clothing or bed linen made from turquoise-colored cloth will also invoke this gem's oasislike qualities. Or take a trip to a desert resort or spa where you can enjoy hot springs and other healing miracles of the earth.*

< 79 >

Emerald ~ 60

Green appears in almost every religion as a symbol of potency and renewal. May Day celebrants in Europe wear green sashes and wreaths, echoing the color of spring. Green was the chosen color of Muhammad and the Islamic color of paradise. Indeed, the value of the emerald lies in its relationship with green, the color of life on our planet. The Koran puts this beautifully in the Pilgrimage: "Do you not see that Allah sends down water from the cloud so the earth becomes green? Surely Allah is Benignant, Aware."

Emeralds are found in Colombia and Africa and elsewhere in South America. Through conquest, trade, and gifting, some of the finest emeralds in the world made their way to Europe. In European heraldry, green represents love, joy, and abundance. The Koran says that in paradise we will wear robes of green silk and live in gardens of perpetuity, beneath which rivers flow. The sixtieth-anniversary couple enjoys a paradise on earth where they and their descendants share the fruits that marriage has sown. As the poet Eugene Field wrote:

> *A little peach in an orchard grew,—*
> *A little peach of emerald hue;*
> *Warmed by the sun and wet by the dew*
> *It grew.*

GIFTS: *On the sixtieth anniversary, the couple takes part in a celebration of the life cycle. Children and grandchildren gather around them with flowers and greenery, according to the season. Gifts can include real emeralds or other green stones with a deep, vibrant hue. (After all, Cleopatra, who loved emeralds, collected mostly green peridots.) A walk or a drive through a forest or a trip to the coast of Ireland provides lovers some time alone in a setting of living green.*

< 80 >

Diamond ~ 65 & 75

The sixty-fifth anniversary is the first of two (the seventy-fifth is also a diamond anniversary) celebrated with diamonds, a symbol of transformation. Like the enduring couple, a diamond takes an incredible journey to become the gem among gems. Diamonds are a form of carbon, one of the most common elements and a component of all living matter on the planet. Miles under the earth's surface, heat, pressure, and time exert tremendous forces to turn carbon into diamond, the hardest and most light-refractive gemstone on earth. Like the carbon that composes 18 percent of our bodies, human beings are also common on this planet. Yet through the processes of time, experience, and love, those who have lived through their sixty-fifth year as a couple are as rare and precious, as resilient and beautiful, as any diamond.

GIFTS: *For the diamond-anniversary couple, vintage diamond jewelry represents value with a sense of history. Or give a gift that symbolizes endurance, with offerings of beautifully presented photo albums or family recordings. For the pair that truly has everything, send monetary gifts on behalf of the couple to their favorite charities.*

< 82 >

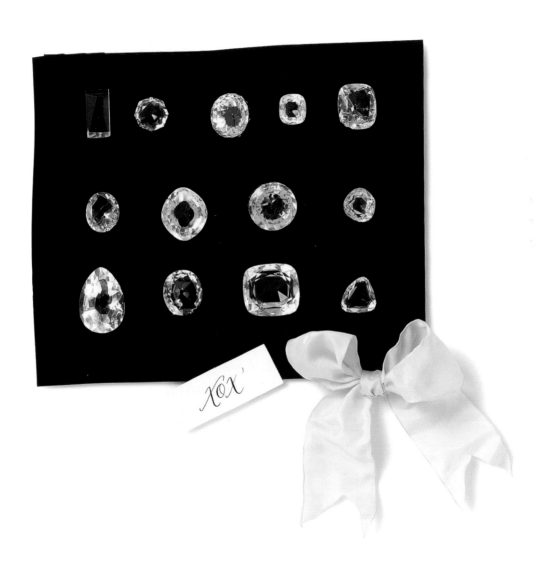

GRÈS. — DIADÈME ET BIJO

Platinum ~ 70

In the scientific realm, platinum is a standard by which to measure things. Until 1960, a platinum-iridium bar also defined the standard for the unit of distance known as the meter. According to the Commission Internationale de l'Éclairage, platinum is still used to define a candela, the unit of luminous intensity that measures intensity of light, or "candlepower." For the seventieth-anniversary couple, platinum is the light of a love that will never tarnish.

Platinum's popularity in jewelry started in the early twentieth century, and has lasted throughout that century and into the next; it is now called the millennium metal. With properties that make it both unobtrusive and imposing, platinum has an elegant history as a foil for gemstones. In Edwardian times, a trendsetting passion for subtle, white-on-white color schemes brought platinum and diamonds together. This trend continued into the Art Deco period, when such famous jewelers as Cartier, Tiffany, and Van Cleef & Arpels designed platinum settings for some of the world's most famous and valuable gemstones. Platinum is known as an "invisible" setting, one that shows off the gem and also keeps it firmly in place. For the couple who has come this far, the bond of matrimony is the setting that has, for seven decades, cradled these two individuals in their places, side by side.

GIFTS: *Antique platinum jewelry, new platinum settings for family diamonds, or a platinum watch will mark this special occasion.*

< 85 >

First	*Paper*	Twenty-seventh	*Sculpture*
Second	*Cotton*	Twenty-eighth	*Orchids*
Third	*Leather*	Twenty-ninth	*Furniture*
Fourth	*Fruits and Flowers*	Thirtieth	*Pearl*
Fifth	*Wood*	Thirty-first	*Timepieces*
Sixth	*Candy*	Thirty-second	*Conveyances*
Seventh	*Wool*	Thirty-third	*Amethyst*
Eighth	*Bronze*	Thirty-fourth	*Opal*
Ninth	*Pottery*	Thirty-fifth	*Jade*
Tenth	*Tin*	Thirty-sixth	*Bone China*
Eleventh	*Steel*	Thirty-seventh	*Alabaster*
Twelfth	*Silk*	Thirty-eighth	*Tourmaline*
Thirteenth	*Lace*	Thirty-ninth	*Lace*
Fourteenth	*Agate*	Fortieth	*Ruby*
Fifteenth	*Crystal*	Forty-first	*Land*
Sixteenth	*Peridot*	Forty-second	*Improved Real Estate*
Seventeenth	*Watches*	Forty-third	*Travel*
Eighteenth	*Cat's-eye*	Forty-fourth	*Literature*
Nineteenth	*Aquamarine*	Forty-fifth	*Sapphire*
Twentieth	*China*	Fiftieth	*Gold*
Twenty-first	*Brass*	Fifty-fifth	*Turquoise*
Twenty-second	*Copper*	Sixtieth	*Emerald*
Twenty-third	*Silver Plate*	Sixty-fifth	*Diamond*
Twenty-fourth	*Musical Instruments*	Seventieth	*Platinum*
Twenty-fifth	*Silver*	Seventy-fifth	*Diamond*
Twenty-sixth	*Original Art*		

< 86 >

RESOURCES

ANTHROPOLOGIE
800-309-2500
www.anthropologie.com
home accessories, tableware, linens

BARNEY'S NEW YORK
888-2BARNEYS
www.barneys.com
clothing, home accessories, tableware, jewelry

CRATE AND BARREL
800-451-8217
www.crateandbarrel.com
furniture, home accessories, tableware, kitchenware, linens

FELISSIMO
800-565-6785
www.felissimo.com
home accessories, jewelry, clothing

THE GARDENER
510-548-4545
furniture, home accessories, tableware

HALLMARK
800-Hallmark
www.hallmark.com
stationery, photo albums

JONATHAN ADLER
877-287-1910
www.jonathanadler.com
home accessories, tableware

POTTERY BARN
800-588-6250
www.potterybarn.com
furniture, home accessories, tableware, kitchenware, linens

REDENVELOPE GIFTS ONLINE
212-350-0100
www.RedEnvelope.com
home accessories, tableware, stationery, jewelry

RESTORATION HARDWARE
800-762-1005
www.restorationhardware.com
furniture, home accessories, tableware, linens

TAKASHIMAYA
212-350-0100
home accessories, tableware, kitchenware

TIFFANY AND COMPANY
800-843-3269
www.tiffany.com
fine jewelry, home accessories

WILLIAMS SONOMA
800-541-2233
www.williams-sonoma.com
tableware, kitchenware, appliances

< 87 >

Acknowledgments

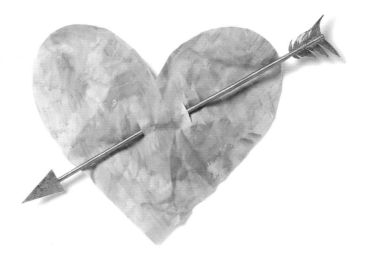

We would like to thank Zoë Francesca for her beautiful and thoughtful workings with the text, and Elvis Swift once again for his perfect calligraphy. Mikyla Bruder gets huge thanks for having the idea in the first place, and she and her assistant Leslie Davisson are both fabulous editors and a joy to work with. Very special thanks also go to Ben Shaykin, Jane Field, Barbara Meyers at Scentiments, Susan Lieberman at Paris 1900, Art Luna, Randy Hild, Constance Brooks, Jon Noble, Clare MacCarley, and Holly Lindem.